Coloured mezzotint by Robert Dighton depicting Toby Fillpot and produced by the London printing firm of Carrington & Bowles in the early 1760s. It was published with an edition of 'The Brown Jug', a song by Francis Fawkes, and probably influenced the development of the Toby jug.

TOBY JUGS
AND RELATED WARES

Graham McLaren

Shire Publications Ltd

CONTENTS

Published in 1994 by Shire Publications Ltd, Cromwell House, Church Street, Princes Risborough, Buckinghamshire HP27 9AA, UK. Copyright © 1994 by Graham McLaren. First edition 1994. Shire Album 310. ISBN 0 7478 0259 9.

Printed in Great Britain by CIT Printing Services, Press Buildings, Merlins Bridge, Haverfordwest, Dyfed SA61 1XF.

British Library Cataloguing in Publication Data: McLaren, Graham. Toby Jugs and Related Wares. – (Shire Albums; No. 310). I. Title II. Series. 738.30942. ISBN 0-7478-0259-9.

ACKNOWLEDGEMENTS

Many people have shown patience and generosity during the preparation of this Album. In particular I would like to thank the following: Valerie Baynton, Stella Beddoe, Diana Lay, Paul Flintoff, Roger Dodsworth, Gordon Elliott, Albert Bowyer, 'Marty', Mary Malone, Richard Slee. The cover photograph is reproduced by courtesy of the Harris Museum and Art Gallery, Preston, Lancashire. Other photographs are acknowledged as follows: the Bass Museum, Burton-upon-Trent, pages 22 (bottom left and right), 26 (bottom); the British Museum, page 1; Broadfield House Glass Museum, Kingswinford, page 31; Harris Museum and Art Gallery, Preston, pages 10, 21 (bottom right), 26 (top left); Roy Kirkham & Company, page 27; Mary Malone, page 21 (bottom left); 'Marty', page 30; Royal Doulton PLC, pages 3, 5 (all), 14 (both), 16 (top right), 17 (bottom), 19 (bottom right), 20 (bottom), 21 (top), 22 (top), 28 (both), 29 (top); the Royal Pavilion, Art Gallery and Museums, Brighton, pages 7, 13 (bottom left), 14 (top left), 15, 16 (both), 17 (top), 18 (both), 19 (top right and bottom left), 20 (top), 24 (bottom right), 25 (all), 26 (top right); Richard Slee, page 32; Staffordshire University, pages 4, 8, 9, 11 (both), 12 (both), 13 (right); Stoke-on-Trent City Museum and Art Gallery, pages 2, 23.

Cover: *'The Sailor' or 'The Planter' type of Toby jug. Staffordshire, late eighteenth or early nineteenth century.*

Below: *Three early Toby variants from the City Museum, Stoke-on-Trent. (Left) 'Sailor' Toby. Probably Staffordshire, late eighteenth century. (Centre) 'Martha Gunn' Toby in Whieldon-type glazes, and showing the distinctive Prince of Wales's feathers. Staffordshire, late eighteenth century or early nineteenth century. (Right) A variation on the Ordinary, 'The Collier'.*

'The Staffordshire Figure Makers', from the series 'Pottery Through the Ages' by Gordon Nicoll for Royal Doulton.

INTRODUCTION

The Toby and the character jugs related to it are today among the most commonly collected forms of ceramics. They are often regarded as having a peculiarly British character and so have drawn the enthusiastic attention of collectors in Britain and elsewhere from the nineteenth century onwards.

Today's form of Toby first appeared as the work of Staffordshire potters during the 1760s. It was the product of a developing pottery industry and a rapidly changing society in Britain. The 'middling classes' were expanding rapidly in number and wealth, demanding items in their homes which moved beyond the strictly functional and towards the decorative. At the same time technical developments allowed potters to be more adventurous in the shapes and styles of their wares than ever before.

The Toby jug prospered in this atmosphere. At first only the 'toper' was represented, the jolly figure dedicated to good food and ale that many would recognise from their local inn. From that form developed images from British society such as the sailor and the parson, and then, as

the eighteenth century gave way to the nineteenth, more specific characters.

Eighteenth-century Toby jugs are today rare and much sought after and are most often to be seen in museum collections. It is the later nineteenth- and twentieth-century types which are most likely to be found in antique shops, collectors' fairs and auctions. Firms such as Royal Doulton have broadened the range of the Toby to include a multitude of 'character jugs' and production of these types has spread throughout Britain and other countries.

Although some political figures have become models for the Toby, it has been dominated throughout its history by characters representing good humour and a pleasantly relaxed lifestyle.

It is probably because of this emphasis that the Toby has been so successful. It moved fairly quickly from being an object which was used (early Toby jugs had removable hats doubling as drinking cups into which the ale would be poured) to being primarily an ornament. Today there is a huge variety of types and sub-types to collect, suiting every purse.

MANUFACTURING TECHNIQUES

The first Toby jugs of the late eighteenth century were made in the Staffordshire potteries by traditional techniques which continued to be used for their manufacture until the end of the nineteenth century. This was partly because the pottery industry has always been slow in adapting to change and partly because the manufacturers of Toby jugs and related wares were small-scale factories or 'shops' which relied on the cheapest forms of hand labour. The large number of poorly decorated nineteenth-century Tobies can be accounted for at least in part by the widespread use of child labour, particularly at the decorating stage of the manufacturing process.

PRESS-MOULDING

The majority of Toby jugs up to the twentieth century were produced in earthenware using the press-moulding process. This technique involves the preparation of a plaster-of-Paris 'master' or 'block-mould' from the original jug modelled in clay. From this, working moulds (also in plaster of Paris) would be made in two, three or more pieces, depending on the complexity of the original model. Thin slabs or 'bats' of damp clay were then laid over the working mould and pressed into its recesses. Excess clay was trimmed away with a knife, and the two halves of the mould were brought together after the edges had been covered with slip (clay of a creamy consistency). The mould would be left for a time while the plaster absorbed some of the moisture from the clay, causing the Toby to shrink and allowing it to be easily released from the mould. Seam-lines and other inconsistencies were removed by hand before the Toby was ready for its first or 'biscuit' firing.

Small intricate elements of clay detail would be moulded separately and stuck to the main form, before the first firing, by 'sprigging', using slip as an adhesive. Many Toby jugs have been named by the presence or absence of small details such

Late eighteenth-century Toby of Ordinary type in the City Museum, Stoke-on-Trent.

as the Prince of Wales's feathers on her cap which identify 'Martha Gunn', for instance.

SLIP-CASTING

Slip-casting began to have a significant impact during the late nineteenth century, when technical advances made the process a viable means of producing large quantities of cheap earthenware and stoneware. Slip-cast Tobies can be identified

4

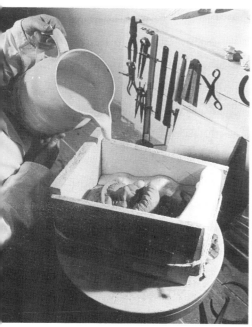

Preparing the block-mould by pouring plaster of Paris over the clay model.

Below: *Extracting the unfired character jug from the working mould.*

The plaster of Paris elements which make up the working mould for Royal Doulton's 'Old Salt' character jug.

Individual elements of complex character jugs are slip-cast separately.

The finished 'Old Salt'. This Royal Doulton character jug has been produced since 1961.

by the even quality of the body, by pinhole marks in the glaze caused by escaping air, and by a slight 'well' or depression at the point where the body of the Toby and its base meet.

The mould-making process was very similar to that of press-moulding, and collectors should be aware that some press-moulds were adapted and used for producing slip-cast replicas into the twentieth century. Slip was poured into the mould and left for approximately twenty minutes. The residue was then poured away, leaving a layer of clay against the side of the mould. Once the clay layer had dried sufficiently in the mould to shrink away from the sides, the Toby was removed and ready for its first firing.

DECORATION AND FIRING

The way in which a Toby has been decorated and fired can reveal much about its possible date and maker. The vast majority of eighteenth- and nineteenth-century Tobies were fired in a lead glaze. More rarely a salt glaze would be used; with this, the orange-peel texture of the thin glaze alone sufficed as decoration.

For lead glazing, underglaze colours (usually a cobalt blue or black) would be applied after the biscuit firing to about 1100°C, and the jug would be fired once again at about 700°C. The glazing or 'glost' firing would be undertaken next, firing to a temperature of about 950°C, which protected the piece with a thin film of glass. The final process (and one often associated with Toby jugs produced from the early nineteenth century onwards) was the application of enamel colours, painted on to the glazed surface. These were mixed with a fluxing agent and fired to about 800°C. The enamelling process was generally more successful with paler, lighter colours. Hence the darker tones of blue and black, used for large surfaces on the Toby, such as his coat or breeches, were usually applied underglaze, with enamels used for the more intricate details.

Variations on the standard methods of decorating Toby jugs include those produced in a syrupy brown-glazed stoneware, known as 'Rockingham' ware, pieces produced in bronze, silver and (more rarely) purple lustres, and Tobies produced in porcelain.

A grotesque face jug in a 'Rockingham' glaze. Mid to late nineteenth century.

A Romano-British cinerary urn in the City Museum, Stoke-on-Trent. First century AD.

THE DEVELOPMENT OF THE TOBY

Although the Toby emerged as a type in Staffordshire during the 1760s, potters throughout the world have since ancient times been making vessels which take their inspiration from the human form. Greek, Roman and indeed medieval British potters created anthropomorphic forms in clay, but the clearest direct ancestor to the Toby was the 'bellarmine' jug or bottle imported into Britain from the middle of the seventeenth century onwards.

This has a bearded face applied as a seal, most often near to the neck of the vessel. These jugs were named after Roberto Bellarmine (1542-1621), a Jesuit cardinal who was disliked as an opponent of Protestantism. Produced first in the Protestant Low Countries and northern Germany, they are an early but significant example of potters making a political statement through their work.

The bellarmine was a highly successful form in Britain and the basic shape was much copied by British potters. Its success was due mostly to the salt-glazed stoneware in which it was made. Sturdy and impervious to most liquids, the imported vessels were far more robust than the lead-glazed earthenware traditionally produced in Britain.

By the early eighteenth century the use of ceramics in Britain had become far more widespread. Social, cultural and economic changes meant that more people could afford decorative items in their homes. Eating and drinking were seen as enjoyable social occasions rather than as necessities. The British pottery industry prospered as it supplied a rapidly expanding market for tableware and decorative accessories.

It was against this background of an increasingly sophisticated society that the Toby form came into being. The printing industry, expanding like many others, brought cheap mass-produced pictures within the reach of potters in Staffordshire and elsewhere, thereby providing the inspiration for the first Toby jugs.

In 1761 the Reverend Francis Fawkes published a song called 'The Brown Jug' as part of his volume of *Original Poems and Translations*. The (very free) translation in this case was from a poem by the sixteenth-century Italian physician Geronimo Amalteo (1507-74) about a

8

character called Gubertus Noricus. The rendition by Fawkes imparts a peculiarly British character to the song, which has as its hero 'Toby Fillpot':

Dear Tom this brown jug that now foams with mild Ale,
(In which I will drink to sweet Nan of the Vale)
Was once Toby Fillpot, a thirsty old Soul
As e'er drank a Bottle or fathom'd a Bowl.
In boozing about 'twas his praise to excel,
And among Jolly Topers he bore off the Bell.

It is highly likely (although not certain) that the success of 'The Brown Jug' was a key element in the development of the Toby. The song was very successful, being republished as a ditty until at least the mid nineteenth century, and it was also published separately by the London printing firm of Carrington & Bowles, accompanied by a coloured mezzotint by Robert Dighton (1752-1812).

Dighton's depiction of a large sprawling toper, foaming beer jug in one hand and pipe in the other, is not exactly copied by any known Toby form from the period. That this is a significant image, however, and one available to Staffordshire potters, is shown by a direct copy. This is an earthenware plaque made by John Turner, a potter working in the Lane End area of the Potteries.

The Dighton toper has a large foaming jug held at the end of an outstretched hand. This would have been difficult to interpret as a vessel, and so it is very possible that the original Toby developed from a combination of imagery such as the Dighton print and the necessities of ceramic production.

Detail of the face and crest from a sixteenth-century German bellarmine in the City Museum, Stoke-on-Trent.

STYLISTIC DEVELOPMENT

The early Toby forms provide the basis for much of what comes afterwards and are the most prized types for the collector. Many of the names and shapes are still in use today.

THE EARLY TYPES, 1770-1810

The jug defined as the 'Ordinary' type by early collectors such as Lord Mackintosh of Halifax is regarded as the standard (and possibly earliest) true Toby form. About 250 mm (10 inches) high, it depicts a corpulent old man seated on an octagonal hollow base. The figure has stringy shoulder-length hair, with heavy unsmiling features and a glazed expression. The mouth is usually slightly open. The figure wears a long coat open at the front, and a scarf or cravat. On his head he wears a tricorn hat. The objects he holds vary, but he is usually balancing a jug of ale on one or other knee. In his other hand he may be carrying a cup (being lifted to his mouth) or a clay pipe. The jug is traditionally associated with the Ralph Wood factory and the design attributed to the French modeller Jean Voyez. There is, however, no absolute evidence for either of these attributions. There is an enormous range of variations on the Ordinary form. Most of them have been given names by collectors, such as the 'Sharp-faced' Toby, the 'Long-faced' Toby, 'The Farrier' (complete with the tools of his trade), the 'Reading' Toby (a rare figure holding an open book) and the 'Step' Toby (named from its step base).

However, the jugs associated with the the cult of the sailor, which was such an aspect of late eighteenth-century British life, may be even earlier than the Ordinary type. Their ancestors are the small mid eighteenth-century 'Midshipman' or 'Midshipmite' jugs, while the early and rare 'Rodney' Toby jugs can be linked to cups inscribed 'Success to Lord Rodney', celebrating the admiral's victory over the French in the West Indies during 1782. Some 'Sailor' jugs form part of the small group of Tobies which can be positively

An undecorated cream-coloured Toby of the Ordinary type. Staffordshire, late eighteenth or early nineteenth century.

attributed to the Wood family; there is an example marked 'WOOD & CALDWELL' in the Victoria and Albert Museum. An interesting 'Sailor' Toby under this name is also known as 'The Planter'. The figure is seated on a chest, often with 'DOLLARS' inscribed on the side, whilst on the jug is occasionally written 'SUCCESS TO OUR WOODEN WALLS'. The maritime attribution is strengthened by the inscription on one example:

Brother Briton
Whoever thou may be
Sit down on
That chest of
Hard dollars by me

And drink a health
To all sailors bold.

The key to its naming lies with the accessories to the figure. If the figure has an anchor it is described as 'The Sailor'; without the anchor but with a plug of tobacco in the left hand, 'The Planter'. This piece cannot be attributed to any particular event, but others are clearly made to commemorate great victories or famous admirals. A rare example, for instance, is the 'Trafalgar Toby' with Nelson's flagship *Victory* impressed on a plaque at the rear. Other early jugs are named after Admiral Howe and Admiral Jervis (Battle of St Vincent, 1797). One of the earliest types of 'Sailor' jug is known as the 'Vernon' after the admiral whose popularity was assured by his victory at Portobello (1739).

'The Squire' is one of the most popular of the early Toby types. This figure sits in a corner chair, smoking a churchwarden pipe and holding a jug. Colouring is typi-

Left: *A rare early 'Fiddler' or 'Midshipmite' jug in the City Museum, Stoke-on-Trent. Staffordshire, mid to late eighteenth century.*
Right: *A 'Rodney' jug in the City Museum, Stoke-on-Trent. Possibly by Ralph Wood, Staffordshire, c.1775.*

11

Left: *An early example of 'The Squire' jug in the City Museum, Stoke-on-Trent. Like many of this type, he has lost his pipe over the years. Staffordshire, late eighteenth century.*
Right: *A 'Sailor' type jug in the City Museum, Stoke-on-Trent. Staffordshire, late eighteenth century.*

cally a dark blue or black coat, green waistcoat and brown hat. The features are well-proportioned, and the figure has straggly shoulder-length hair. The type has been produced into the twentieth century by firms such as William Kent of Burslem, and Royal Doulton has produced a variation of the type. It has also been widely faked, particularly during the late nineteenth century. This is a fate it shares with the 'Shield' Toby, a very rare type.

It is named after the usually green, shield-shaped cartouche impressed 'IT IS ALL OUT, THEN FILL IT AGIAN' [*sic*].

Like 'The Squire' and 'The Shield', 'The Thin Man' is often attributed to the Ralph Wood factory and sometimes considered to be a very early Toby prototype. The figure sits in an unusually ornate chair, feet resting on a raised rectangular step. The slightly curly hair is longer than normal, tumbling down over the shoulders.

Whilst all of these Tobies are depicted seated, in the Ordinary tradition, there are also many standing types. 'The Snufftaker' is an extremely popular form, produced by many potters. It is probably the most common of the standing types and was made throughout the nineteenth and twentieth centuries. It is found in a number of glaze and body types including the dark brown Rockingham glaze and a cream-coloured earthenware body associated with the Davenport factory. The type is sometimes suggested to be a depiction of Benjamin Franklin, although there is no proof of this attribution.

Far rarer, and arguably more impressive, is the 'Falstaff' jug, a standing type described by the early twentieth-century ceramic historian Frank Falkner as 'probably the finest earthenware jug ever made in early Staffordshire days'. Also known

Below: *A large 'Rodney' type jug. Staffordshire, late eighteenth century.*

Above: *A 'Thin Man' jug in the City Museum, Stoke-on-Trent. Staffordshire, late eighteenth century.*

13

as 'The Prince of Wales', 'Prince Hal' and 'Bluff King Hal', it may represent an early attempt to re-create the 'Sir Toby Belch' character. There are two main types, both of which are among the largest of the late eighteenth-century Tobies, standing between 380 and 460 mm (15 and 18 inches) high. In one the figure holds a wine cup in one hand, a flagon in the other. The other type holds a sword in the right hand, a cudgel behind his back in the left hand. This latter figure is normally attributed to the Wood factory. The archaic dress suggests it is a very early example of the makers of Toby jugs taking inspiration from the theatre. It has also been suggested (without evidence) that it depicts the Prince of Wales masquerading as Henry VIII at a Brighton ball.

The possible Brighton connection is continued by 'Martha Gunn', a type of female Toby jug highly prized by collectors. An example of this type fetched £630 at auction as early as 1919. 'Martha Gunn' is named after the Brighton bathing attendant who tended the Prince of Wales (later George IV):

Standing Toby, early to mid nineteenth century.

The Falstaff character jug designed by Harry Fenton for Doulton and introduced in 1950. This jug continues a tradition of representing this character which dates back to the eighteenth century.

An early nineteenth-century 'Martha Gunn' type holding cup and bottle, decorated in Pratt ware colours, with cap in foreground.

To Brighton came he,
Came George III's son,
To be dipped in the sea
By famed Martha Gunn.

This Toby is often identified by the feathers on her hat. Variations, in which the model holds a gin bottle or a foaming ale jug, are known as 'The Gin Woman' and 'Drunken Sal'. 'Martha Gunn' is often attributed to Ralph Wood, but there would also seem to be strong links (particularly for 'Drunken Sal') with the Davenport factory, which produced female Tobies from about 1830 onwards. Variants on the type were produced throughout the early nineteenth century at various centres, including Yorkshire.

While figures like 'The Gin Woman' hint at the darker side of eighteenth-century drinking, 'The Hearty Good Fellow' suggests only jovial good nature. Also known as 'The Old English Gentleman', this standing Toby is usually associated with the Walton factory because there is a marked specimen in the British Museum. The figure stands in a long coat with the left arm thrown across the chest. In the right hand he holds either a foam-

A late 'Martha Gunn' type jug with sponged and enamel decoration. By this stage the type had lost the distinctive Prince of Wales's feathers marking its link with Regency Brighton. Perhaps Staffordshire, 1820-40.

ing jug or a cup. Other details, such as the colouring of his coat and breeches, can vary. There is evidence that this model was produced by other manufacturers, including Lakin and Poole.

The final category of early Toby can be associated with religion.

The rich country parson, who lived well, was a familiar theme in late eighteenth-century popular culture. Variations of the jug can be found either seated or standing. The standing version is often known as 'The Parson of the Tithe Pig Group' and is related to a Staffordshire earthenware group depicting the collecting of the annual tithe. In this, the parson is being offered the tenth child of the family rather than the tenth pig.

The jug sometimes has an inscription: 'I will have no child tho the X pig'. The seated 'Parson' jug is a variation of the Ordinary model, pouring drink unevenly into a glass, and wearing a full-length clerical wig. The jug is also rather confusingly known as 'The Unfrocked Parson' when the coat is coloured instead of black, and it has also been described as 'Dr Johnson' by collectors.

An example of 'The Hearty Good Fellow' type. Staffordshire, late eighteenth or early nineteenth century.

An apparently related figure is 'The Nightwatchman', a much copied type, despite being rather impractical. The model has no hat, and so the opening for the liquid is at the back. Usually found decorated in overglaze enamels, the figure has a white wig and is sitting in a high-backed chair, holding a lamp in his right hand. The original is often attributed to Enoch Wood, although many copies exist. Some have suggested that this figure does not represent a nightwatchman at all, but the famous eighteenth-century preacher George Whitefield, parodied in Joseph Reed's 1761 play *The Register Office* as 'Mr Watchlight'.

'The Landlord' or 'The Publican'. Perhaps Staffordshire, early nineteenth century.

LATER TYPES

During the nineteenth century there was a huge expansion in the range of Toby jugs and related wares which paralleled an expansion of the pottery trade generally. A new range of Tobies was developed which were modelled on particular characters drawn from literature, the stage and elsewhere. During this period enamelling was applied wholeheartedly to the Toby form. This improved technology, together with the availability of designs to be copied, resulted in identifiable characters, rather than generic types representing general good humour and 'Toperism'. Types of Toby intended entirely for decoration were developed, such as the miniatures, and later still the 'tinies' produced by Doulton and other companies.

Literary and theatrical characters provided a new resource for Toby modellers, the greatest number originating from the works of Charles Dickens. Characters like Mr Pickwick, Micawber and Sairey Gamp

Mr Pickwick character jug by Doulton, produced between 1948 and 1960.

Above: *'Punch', mid nineteenth century.*

ing the bicentenary of the writer's birth. He was later reproduced as a character jug in the 1950s, also by Doulton.

Technical advances such as enamelling also benefited the production of military figures. The collector of eighteenth-century Toby jugs struggles to attribute different types to particular heroes. From the nineteenth century, however, a range of military Tobies exists, providing evidence of the popularity of this type. Foremost amongst these are the triumvirate of Nelson, Wellington and Napoleon, who

Below: *'John Bull'. Marked 'registered no 153475'. This type is known to have been manufactured by William Kent & Company of Burslem during the late nineteenth century.*

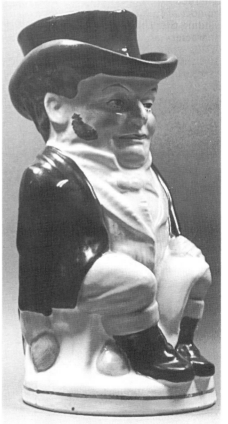

have featured again and again as character jugs by a variety of Toby makers.

Toby jugs with a theatrical theme can arguably be traced back as far as the famous 'Falstaff' jug. The availability of illustrated songsheets and playbills provided valuable material for the designers of Toby jugs from an early stage. Jugs such as the standing Toby of 'Paul Pry' based on the comic character created by John Liston in 1825 are evidence of the popularity of the theatre by the early nineteenth century.

By the twentieth century the popularity of the Toby was so vast that it had been produced in some form by almost every British pottery manufacturer and in every significant pottery-making district. The development by Royal Doulton and other firms of the 'character jug' opened a new stage in the history of the Toby type, hugely extending the range of shapes and forms.

One of the earliest 'character' pieces produced by the Lambeth works of Doulton was a salt-glaze stoneware spirit flask of Samuel Johnson modelled by Leslie Harradine in 1909, commemorat-

were produced throughout the century in a number of body types (including porcelain) and glazes, such as the dark brown Rockingham ware.

Most impressive are the early character jugs by the Lambeth works of the Doulton company. From the 1820s a variety was produced in salt-glazed stoneware in a range of sizes. Some, such as the large character jug of Nelson, are examples of high technical skill because of the intricate detailing of the uniform and insignia, requiring careful modelling and firing. They rank among the finest examples of ceramic 'sculpture' to be produced during the first half of the nineteenth century. Because of the success of the Doulton enterprise its products were imitated by a number of Lambeth salt-glaze potters, including Stephen Green, who produced a character jug of Napoleon during the 1820s which is well-known to collectors. The value of the character jug as a commemorative piece resulted in the popu-

The Duke of Wellington as a character jug decorated in both underglaze and overglaze colours. Probably Staffordshire, c.1820-40.

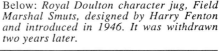

Below: *Royal Doulton character jug, Field Marshal Smuts, designed by Harry Fenton and introduced in 1946. It was withdrawn two years later.*

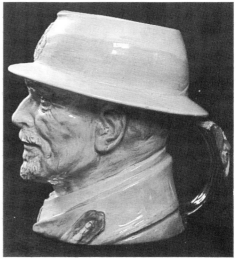

Above: *Doulton & Watts salt-glaze stoneware figure jug depicting Nelson. Lambeth, c.1830.*

Examples of Napoleon and Wellington character jugs in salt-glaze stoneware. Lambeth, mid nineteenth century.

larity of military jugs continuing into the twentieth century. F. Carruthers Gould, for instance, produced a range which included representations of Earl Haig, Kitchener and Smuts for the Royal Stafford Pottery during the First World War.

The development of the 'political' Toby seems to have been part of a general politicisation of British society which took place from the second quarter of the nineteenth century onwards. The salt-glaze stoneware spirit flasks of the 1820s onwards are direct relations of the Toby and include representations of such figures as Queen Caroline, the young Victoria (in white stoneware) and later her consort, Prince Albert. The furore surrounding the Reform Bill (1832), in particular, brought about the creation of political figures such as that of Lord Brougham, who was influential in promoting the bill, made by Joseph Bourne of Denby during the 1830s.

Nineteenth-century political Tobies include the rare 'William Gladstone' by Sampson Smith of about 1870. During the twentieth century Sir Winston Churchill would seem to be the most popular political personality for the character-jug designers, being 'Tobied' by a wide variety of manufacturers including Royal

Three salt-glaze stoneware 'reform flasks'. (Left and right) Lord Brougham. (Centre) William IV. Doulton & Watts, Lambeth, 1832.

A range of brown stoneware spirit flasks designed by Leslie Harradine and made by Doulton (Lambeth) between 1908 and 1911. (From left to right) Lord Balfour, Lord Haldane, John Burns, Herbert Asquith, David Lloyd George, Austen Chamberlain.

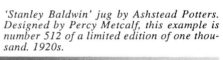

'Stanley Baldwin' jug by Ashstead Potters. Designed by Percy Metcalf, this example is number 512 of a limited edition of one thousand. 1920s.

Original clay model for 'Margaret Thatcher', a character jug manufactured by Roy Kirkham & Company, 1979.

The Toby jug as a symbol of tradition and jovial good humour has become so ingrained in the British consciousness that it is only natural that advertisers should make use of its positive image. The Toby form has been used by a number of distilleries as a 'limited edition' container for their whisky. A good example is the 'McCallum' character jug representing a highlander made for the distillers of the same name by Doulton during the 1930s. The best-known use of the Toby for advertising, however, is that associated with the brewing industry. The first company to use the Toby as a symbol was probably Hoare's Brewery, which registered the Toby label in 1907, although it had been in use for many years before that. The merger of Hoare's and Charrington in 1933 led to its use nationally as both a trademark and 'in the round', with Toby jugs being made for the brewery by manufacturers including Wade and Beswick.

Doulton. A particularly collectable example is by the famous designer Clarice Cliff for Wilkinsons in 1941. More recently, politicians personified in the form of character jugs have included Margaret Thatcher (Roy Kirkham) and Ronald Reagan (Royal Doulton).

Charrington advertising Toby and associated placard, 1965-89. Marked 'Wade Regina'.

Charrington advertising Toby in Ordinary form. Wood & Sons of Burslem, 1935-65.

22

THE TOBY MANUFACTURERS

A Wood-type Toby jug of the Ordinary form. Staffordshire, late eighteenth century.

The identification and attribution of early Tobies is notoriously difficult. Very few are marked, and even those which are impressed with a name can confuse rather than clarify the true identity of the maker. For instance, some writers on the Toby jug have made much of the significance of the early Stoke potters Astbury and Whieldon in the development of the type. There is, however, very little evidence to support this, and only the generic term 'Astbury-Whieldon' survives to describe a particular quality of mottled underglaze decoration used on some eighteenth-century Toby jugs.

Similar confusion surrounds the contribution of the Wood family, a Staffordshire concern which began in the eighteenth century and continued as an independent manufacturer until recently. Ralph Wood I (1715-72) and Ralph Wood II are credited with bringing about something of a revolution in the making of pottery figures and are seen by many as being the true 'fathers' of the Toby. Marked specimens of the Ordinary, 'Falstaff' and other Toby types are known. They are signed 'Ra Wood', 'Ra. Wood Burslem' and 'R. WOOD' (although much forging of these names has been recorded).

Many have supposed that it is possible to differentiate between the work of the younger and elder Ralph by the differences of signature, but this remains pure supposition. Indeed, recent evidence suggests that the brother of Ralph Wood II, John Wood Senior (1743-97), was more significant as a manufacturer of Tobies. The confusion surrounding these early Wood types demonstrates that many factors have to be taken into account when attempting to attribute early Tobies to particular makers.

The contribution of Enoch Wood (1759-1840) is somewhat clearer. He was a skilled modeller (his bust of John Wesley is famous) and had been apprenticed to both Josiah Wedgwood and Humphrey Palmer. An inveterate collector of both pottery and printed ephemera (part of his collection and his scrapbooks survive in the City Museum, Stoke-on-Trent), his main contribution to the development of the Toby type seems to have been a much greater emphasis on enamel decoration. He also developed the earlier forms and introduced new types such as 'Paul Pry' and 'The Nightwatchman'.

The romantic associations of the Wood family name can be beguiling, and yet other potters appear equally capable of producing original high-quality types. A good example of this in terms of technical quality is the work of James Neale, who was in business from 1778, later entering into partnership with Robert Wilson. It has been argued that the quality of his enamelling was superior to that of the Woods, using bright colours to great effect. At the same time we know that Enoch Wood was supplying some of the moulds for his figures. The marked pieces

23

tend to be of the Ordinary type, owing much to the original model. Another marked Neale type is 'The Collier'.

More original in design terms was John Walton, to whom are attributed 'The American Sailor' as well as 'The Hearty Good Fellow'. His Tobies are notable for a sculptural treatment which gives them a character akin to contemporary porcelain. He seems to have produced Tobies during the first quarter of the nineteenth century, but again firm attribution is dangerous as there were several potters named Walton working in the Stoke-on-Trent area at that time.

The Toby jugs created by John Davenport are part of a huge range of ceramics and glass produced by this Longport potter, whose business lasted from 1793 to 1876. The best-known type is probably the 'Drunken Sal', but a rarer example known as the 'Four-cornered Hat' Toby is also recorded. All Davenport Tobies are decorated with good enamel decoration. Unusually, many are also signed and dated, and so it is known that the production of Tobies by the Davenport concern was largely concentrated between 1830 and 1850.

Whilst some Tobies can be attributed

Left: *A variation of 'The Hearty Good Fellow' type. Early nineteenth century.*
Right: *The 'Cross-legged' Toby, also known as 'The Jolly Miller'. Probably Davenport, c.1840.*

24

Left: *Standing Toby in Pratt ware colours, early to mid nineteenth century.*
Right: *Two examples of 'The Snufftaker'. The example on the right is in a 'Rockingham' glaze. Mid to late nineteenth century.*

to particular manufacturers, others come under general 'type' headings. One of the most distinctive types is that associated with Felix Pratt (1780-1859). Using high-temperature underglaze colours with an emphasis on blues and yellows, the decoration often crudely applied with a sponge, this type was produced in various parts of Britain, including Newcastle upon Tyne and Scotland. As a result it has earned the generic term of 'Pratt ware'. It is almost impossible to ascribe the many types of Toby which are decorated with Pratt ware colours to Felix Pratt himself as so few are signed.

A similar fate has befallen the 'Rockingham' name, associated originally with the Swinton factory in South Yorkshire founded during the 1780s. The rich, syrupy brown glaze was applied to many Toby forms, particularly from the 1840s onwards. Amongst Toby types, 'The

Snufftaker' and 'The Gin Woman' are commonly found in a Rockingham-type glaze.

Brown stoneware had been made in Derbyshire since the eighteenth century, but it was only with early nineteenth-century technical improvements, particularly in firing processes, that Brampton became known for producing a wide range of salt-glazed pieces including Toby jugs. The quality of these improved yet further during the nineteenth century and this, together with the fact that many are named and therefore attributable to particular manufacturers, has made them popular with collectors.

By the mid nineteenth century hundreds of potteries, large and small, were producing Toby jugs or their variants. The Toby had become a nationally produced item; and this trend has continued. Areas particularly associated with the design and

25

Left: *The 'Squat' Toby. Probably Spode, late nineteenth century.*
Right: *Salt-glaze stoneware Toby of Ordinary form. Unmarked, but probably Brampton, Derbyshire, c.1835-40.*

Worthington advertising jugs by Beswick, probably 1950s.

A range of character jugs manufactured by Roy Kirkham & Company, Tunstall, 1980s.

production of Toby jugs include Swansea and Leeds, where potters had been producing cream-coloured earthenware of a quality to rival Staffordshire from the mid eighteenth century onwards. Some writers argue that certain early types originate in Leeds rather than Staffordshire.

ROYAL DOULTON

The development of the Toby type during the eighteenth and nineteenth centuries was achieved through the contribution of various firms, but the productions

of Doulton have led the way during the twentieth century. Most significant was the development of the character jug from 1934 onwards by the company's chief designer, Charles J. Noke.

Founded by John Doulton (1793-1873), Doulton had been producing character jugs from the 1820s, most notably in salt-glaze stoneware at their Lambeth factory. In design terms though, the twentieth-century character jug was developed from the 'whole-face' types. These have their basis in the late nineteenth-century work

Slip-cast salt-glaze jugs designed by Harry Simeon for Doulton. (Left) 'Before and After Marriage'. (Right) 'Double XX'. Lambeth, 1924-30.

of art potters such as the Martin Brothers, who worked in Lambeth and benefited from technical assistance from Doulton. Between 1910 and 1930 the Doulton factory produced some seated Tobies in salt glaze, and later, under the instigation of Harry Simeon, a larger range which included coloured types. The development of character jugs such as 'John Barleycorn' (1934) heralded a further development of the Staffordshire tradition of the Toby jug, however. The vastly increased colour range available to the twentieth-century potter and the intricate modelling allowed by the slip-casting process have enabled Royal Doulton to build up a vast range of character jugs and related wares, with an enthusiastic following of collectors. Features have been gradually introduced, such as the integrated design of the handle (with 'Sairey Gamp' in 1935), speciality pieces such as napkin rings, and even cigarette lighters in 'character' form. Limited edition jugs and those which had a short production life tend to be the most collectable; Sir Jimmy

Saville's example of 'Toby Gillette', made in a limited edition of three for the *Jim'll Fix It* television programme, fetched £15,000 when sold at auction.

'John Barleycorn', designed by Charles Noke for Doulton in 1934, and in production until 1960.

THE LAWYER　　　　　CAPT. AHAB　　　　　THE MIKADO

VIKING　　　　　BACCHUS　　　　　THE FORTUNE TELLER

A range of character jugs introduced by Doulton c.1960.

A grotesque face jug by the Martin Brothers in brown stone-ware, c.1895.

THE TOBY IN AMERICA AND EUROPE

Although the Toby jug is often characterised as 'typically British' or even 'typically English', it has been produced by many potteries around the world. During the nineteenth century American potteries such as Lenox, Bennington and Syracuse produced both Toby jugs and, more usually, character jugs. These tend to be related to particular personalities and events such as the Washington and Roosevelt jugs modelled by Isaac Broome and produced by Lenox (1896 and 1909).

In Europe the trend has been to develop the Toby type rather than to copy the British original. Manufacturing was, and is, widespread, with firms in France, Spain, Portugal and elsewhere producing allied types. A particularly interesting example is the Sarreguemines Pottery, near Strasbourg in France. This produced a wide variety of character jugs during the late nineteenth and early twentieth centuries. Decorated in majolica style, they were a conscious attempt to repeat the success of British types. Nevertheless, in the bright colours and subtle variations of decoration they succeed in creating a unique effect.

A private collection of character jugs by the French Sarreguemines factory and dating from the period 1895-1910.

FURTHER READING

Atterbury, Paul. *English Pottery and Porcelain, An Historical Survey*. Peter Owen, 1980.

Bedford, John. *Toby Jugs*. Cassell, 1968.

Eyles, Desmond. *Good Sir Toby*. Doulton & Company, 1955.

Eyles, Desmond. *The Doulton Lambeth Wares*. Hutchinson, 1975.

Eyles, Desmond. *Character Jugs and Toby Jugs*. Royal Doulton, 1979.

Halfpenny, Pat. *English Earthenware Figures 1740-1840*. Antique Collectors Club, 1991.

Honey, William B. *The Art of the Potter*. Faber & Faber, 1956.

Hughes, G. Bernard. *English and Scottish Earthenware 1660-1860*. Lutterworth Press, 1961.

Lockett, Terry A., and Godden, Geoffrey A. *Davenport China, Earthenware and Glass 1794-1887*. Barrie & Jenkins, 1989.

Oliver, Anthony. *Staffordshire Pottery – The Tribal Art of England*. Heinemann, 1981.

Paton, James. *Jugs: A Collector's Guide*. Souvenir Press, 1976.

Rackham, Bernard. *Early Staffordshire Pottery*. Faber & Faber, 1951.

Rhead, G. Woolicroft. *The Earthenware Collector*. Herbert Jenks, 1920.

Schuler, Vic. *Toby Jugs*. Kevin Francis, 1986.

Sotheby & Company. *The Mackintosh Collection of Fine Toby Jugs*. Auction Catalogue, May 1967.

Turner, H. A. B. *A Collector's Guide to Staffordshire Pottery Figures*. MacGibbon & Kee, 1971.

A very unusual example of a Toby of Ordinary form in mould-blown lead glass. British, mid twentieth century.

PLACES TO VISIT

Intending visitors are advised to find out the hours of opening and whether relevant items are on display before making a special journey.

Ashmolean Museum of Art and Archaeology, Beaumont Street, Oxford OX1 2PH. Telephone: 01865 278000.

The Bass Museum, Horninglow Street, Burton-upon-Trent, Staffordshire DE14 1JZ. Telephone: 01283 42031 or 511000.

The British Museum, Great Russell Street, London WC1B 3DG. Telephone: 0171-636 1555.

Castle Museum, The Castle, Nottingham NG1 6EL. Telephone: 01602 483504.

Harris Museum and Art Gallery, Market Square, Preston, Lancashire PR1 2PP. Telephone: 01772 258248.

John Beswick Studio, Gold Street, Longton, Stoke-on-Trent, Staffordshire ST3 2JP. Telephone: 01782 292292.

National Museum of Wales, Cathays Park, Cardiff, South Glamorgan CF1 3NP. Telephone: 01222 397951.

Royal Museum of Scotland, Chambers Street, Edinburgh EH1 1JF. Telephone: 0131-225 7534.

The Royal Pavilion, 4/5 Pavilion Buildings, Brighton, East Sussex BN1 1UE. Telephone: 01273 603005.

Stoke-on-Trent City Museum and Art Gallery, Bethesda Street, Hanley, Stoke-on-Trent, Staffordshire ST1 3DE. Telephone: 01782 202173.

Victoria and Albert Museum, Cromwell Road, South Kensington, London SW7 2RL. Telephone: 0171-938 8500.

'Young Toby' by Richard Slee, 1993. An ironic treatment of the tradition of the Toby jug by one of Britain's leading studio potters.